THE PINK BOOK

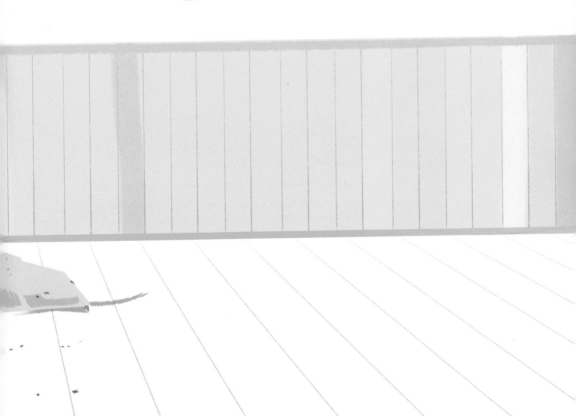

For Zenta
—D.M.

Text copyright © 2020 by Diane Muldrow

Cover and interior illustrations copyright © 2020 by Mike Yamada

All rights reserved. Published in the United States by Random House Children's Books,
a division of Penguin Random House LLC, New York.

Random House and the colophon and Beginner Books and colophon are registered trademarks
of Penguin Random House LLC. The Cat in the Hat logo ® and © Dr. Seuss Enterprises, L.P.
1957, renewed 1986. All rights reserved.

Visit us on the Web!
rhcbooks.com

Educators and librarians, for a variety of teaching tools, visit us at RHTeachersLibrarians.com

Library of Congress Cataloging-in-Publication Data is available upon request.

ISBN 978-1-9848-5019-5 (trade) — ISBN 978-1-9848-5020-1 (lib. bdg.)
ISBN 978-1-9848-5021-8 (ebook)

MANUFACTURED IN CHINA
10 9 8 7 6 5 4 3 2 1
First Edition

THE PINK BOOK

by DIANE MULDROW
illustrated by MIKE YAMADA

BEGINNER BOOKS®
A Division of Random House

Put red and white together—
and what do they do?
They make PINK—my favorite hue!

Welcome to my world—my world of PINK!

There's just no color like

PINK,

I think!

It comes in shades of every kind.
Let's see how many we can find!

Piggy pink,

blush pink,
carnation pink, too!

Melon,

taffy,

bubblegum—

any pink will do!

The stripes in a sunset?

The inside of a shell?

Pearly pink is a color

I know very well!

Pink is the color of unicorn hair,
and the color of frilly underwear!

Pink are the brine shrimp
that flamingos eat.
The shrimp turn them pink
from their heads to their feet!

Coral dots,
a peachy stripe,

hot pink snowboard—
hello, half-pipe!

Grow it!
Throw it!

Slap it on the wall!

Wear it!

Share it!

Roll it in a ball!

When I become president,
the first thing I'll do
is paint the White House
a rosier hue!

Pink is a leaf.

Pink is a place.

Pink is a gem.

Pink is a face.

Pink you can eat.

Pink you can drink.

Pink you can ride.

Pink you can blink.

Pink flowers.

Pink nails.

Pink ice cream.

Pink snails.

I'm bonkers,
I'm zonkers
for PINK!

Pink is a hot dog thrown on the grill!

Pink is the medicine I take when I'm ill!

Pink can be as soft as a baby's toes . . .

and as cozy as the coat I wear when it snows.

Pink can shimmer.
Pink can glimmer.

It can be soft

or bright,
more red
or more white.

Yellow is nice and so is blue,
but for me,
only PINK will do!

STONE ARCH BOOKS
a capstone imprint

⋎⋏ STONE ARCH BOOKS™

Published in 2014 by Stone Arch Books
A Capstone Imprint
1710 Roe Crest Drive
North Mankato, MN 56003
www.capstonepub.com

Originally published by DC Comics in the U.S. in single
magazine form as Batman: Li'l Gotham.
Copyright © 2014 DC Comics. All Rights Reserved.

DC Comics
1700 Broadway, New York, NY 10019
A Warner Bros. Entertainment Company
Printed in China.
032014   008085LEOF14

Cataloging-in-Publication Data is available at the Library
of Congress website:
ISBN: 978-1-4342-9220-9 (library binding)

Summary: April showers bring...Mr. Freeze? When the
coldhearted super-villain is granted his freedom from
Arkham Asylum, he is welcomed back into Gotham City
with open arms. But Gotham's warm embrace will turn to
a cold reception if Batman can't stop him. Then, on Cinco
de Mayo, Damian Wayne, Batman's son, leads his friends
into battle with the seedy underworld of street racing,
cage wrestling, and back-alley taco-eating competitions!
Each library bound book in this action packed series
features a comics glossary, visual discussion questions,
and writing prompts.

STONE ARCH BOOKS
Ashley C. Andersen Zantop **Publisher**
Michael Dahl **Editorial Director**
Sean Tulien **Editor**
Heather Kindseth **Creative Director**
Bob Lentz **Art Director**
Hilary Wacholz **Designer**
Kathy McColley **Production Specialist**

DC Comics
Sarah Gaydos & Kristy Quinn **Original U.S. Editors**

APRIL SHOWERS AND CINCO DE MAYO

Dustin Nguyen & Derek Fridolfs....................... writers

Dustin Nguyen.. artist

Saida Temofonte... letterer

BATMAN created by
Bob Kane

MR. FRIES, YOU'VE MADE REMARKABLE PROGRESS AND ARE NO LONGER REQUIRED TO STAY.

VICTOR, I'M PLEASED TO TELL YOU... YOU'RE FREE TO GO.

HEYA, VIC! YOU'RE LEAVING US ALREADY? GOOD FOR YOU, BUD.

ALSO I WANTED TO THANK YA FOR YOUR CONCERNS OVER MY SICK GIRL.

IF YOU'LL FOLLOW ME, I'LL WALK YOU OUT.

PLEASE, GIVE THIS TO YOUR DAUGHTER. I HOPE SUZI FEELS BETTER SOON.

SNIFF

FREEDOM!

GOTHAM CITY TRANSIT

ALL ABOARD! NEXT STOP, GOTHAM CITY.

YIP YIP

GULP!

YOU CAN HAVE MY SEAT.

HERE, TAKE MINE.

I'LL MAKE ROOM FOR YOU HERE, SIR.

YOU CAN SIT NEXT TO ME, YOUNG MAN. PICKLES HERE DOESN'T MIND, DO YOU, PICKLES?

YIP YIP

IS IT POSSIBLE? EVERYONE IS SO KIND. SO NICE.

HAS THE CITY REALLY CHANGED THIS MUCH SINCE I'VE BEEN AWAY?

"ONE LITTLE SNOWMAN WAITED FOR THE BUS."

"HE CLIMBED UP THE STAIRS TO GO REJOIN US."

SSHH! TAKEN!

GRRR... TAKEN!

BOTH ARE TAKEN!

"ALONG CAME THE SUN AND SHONE ALL DAY.

"AND ONE LITTLE SNOWMAN MELTED AWAY."

TIME FOR THIS FLOWER TO BLOOM OUTTA HERE. LATER, FREEZY POPS!

HELLO, LITTLE SNOWMAN. WINTER HAS RETURNED.

ON YOUR MARKERS, FELLAS...

...READY, GET SET...

GOTHAM, THE BOWERY.

...MOVE IT!!

VROOOM!

RRRRROOOOWWW

SCREEEEECH!

MAAAN...*EVERYONE'S* INTO DRIFTING THESE DAYS, BUT THIS IS WHERE IT'S AT, MAN. THE TRUE TEST OF THE MACHINE.

NO WAY. DRIFTING'S ALL ABOUT THE DRIVER! THAT'S WHERE THE TRUE TEST IS--*SKILLZ!*

THAT'S WHERE REACTION TIME COMES INTO PLAY THOUGH, SEE...

DO WE NEED TO GO OVER THE PLAN AGAIN?

HERE COMES COLIN!

DAMIAN. *DAMIAN!*

YEAH, YEAH. FIND BANE. FOLLOW HIM BACK TO HIS WAREHOUSE. CALL NIGHTWING. BUST HIM FOR HIS ILLEGAL WARES. *GOTCHA.*

VROOO

CREATORS

DUSTIN NGUYEN — CO-WRITER & ILLUSTRATOR

Dustin Nguyen is an American comic artist whose body of work includes Wildcats v3.0, The Authority Revolution, Batman, Superman/Batman, Detective Comics, Batgirl, and his creator owned project Manifest Eternity. Currently, he produces all the art for Batman: Li'l Gotham, which is also written by himself and Derek Fridolfs. Outside of comics, Dustin moonlights as a conceptual artist for toys, games, and animation. In his spare time, he enjoys sleeping, driving, and sketching things he loves.

DEREK FRIDOLFS — CO-WRITER

Derek Fridolfs is a comic book writer, inker, and artist. He resides in Gotham--present and future.

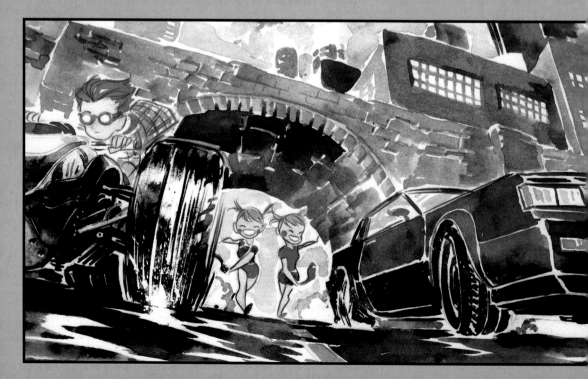

GLOSSARY

arsenal (ARSS-uhn-uhl)--a collection of weapons

concerns (con-SERNZ)--worries or issues that need to be addressed

conversion (kuhn-VER-zhuhn)--the process of changing from one thing to another

dialogue (DYE-uh-log)--conversation or speech

cure (KYOOR)--a method or period of medical treatment

decency (DEE-sen-see)--the quality or state of being good

ironic (i-RON-ik)--if you say something that is ironic, the words mean the opposite of what you intended

gridlocked (GRID-lockd)--a traffic standstill

intent (in-TENT)--intention or purpose

pristine (priss-TEEN)--being fresh and clean

progress (PROG-ress)--gradual improvement or advancement

stardust (STAR-dust)--dusty material found between the stars

VISUAL QUESTIONS & PROMPTS

1. Which Robin do you like better: Damian [bottom] or Tim [top]? Why?

2. Who is Catwoman talking to? Why is she watching Nightwing and Oracle?

3. Why do you think Batman follows Mr. Freeze the minute he's released from prison?

4. Several characters have special vehicles in this book. Whose vehicle would you want for yourself? Why?

READ THEM ALL!

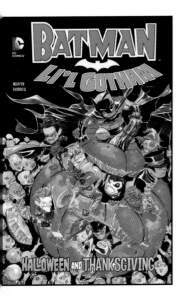